HIS LIFE WAS LOST

Christy M.

Order this book online at www.trafford.com
or email orders@trafford.com

Most Trafford titles are also available at major online book retailers.

Printed in the United States of America.

ISBN: 978-1-4269-5858-8 (sc)
ISBN: 978-1-4269-5859-5 (e)

Trafford rev. 03/11/2011

 www.trafford.com

North America & international
toll-free: 1 888 232 4444 (USA & Canada)
phone: 250 383 6864 ♦ fax: 812 355 4082

HIS LIFE WAS LOST.

He lived his life to the fullest of no time at all. Jr. was the light of my life and all of my hopes and dreams to start a family when he arrived in this world. I was waiting with open arms to give him life and for all my dreams to come true.

To have my first son and have a family that I could call mine.

To be proud of something for once in my life. The day he was born he would change my life forever. I had lived an abused life for most of my life and was lost in the world of drugs but when I found out that I was pregnant with Jr.. I wanted to change my life for him because the baby meant more to me then the fast life of drugs and alcohol.

I wanted nothing more than to have a family because I never knew what family was. I never had one. My son was the best thing that ever happened to me.

Jr. was a joyful child growing up. He liked mostly to have him playing with other children. His personality was many ways but he was never selfish and always got along with others. I gave birth to three other children and Jr. was there to help take care of the babies. He was most happy when his sister was born. Jr. loved her more than anything and was very protective over her and did everything for her. In 2004 Jr. wanted to take a trip to North Carolina with his grandparents. I really didn't want him to go because I don't let my children leave without me because I know in my heart that anything can happen. I decided after a couple of days to let Jr. go on the trip. Jr. was gone for five days. He was calling me on the phone three or more times a day to let me know that he was ok. Talking to Jr. I could tell that he was having a good time and he was enjoying his self. I was very happy that Jr. was enjoying his self but my heart was crushed that he was gone because this was my first time without him.

When Jr. returned home after five days in North Carolina I was relieved and very excited to see him and hold him. This was the first time Jr. has ever left my side in ten years.

I knew that I had to let loose some time but that was very hard for me to do.

My children meant the world to me and I feel that I was blessed with them and they were giving to me for a reason and no matter what I was going to perfect them no matter what I had to do and I was never going to let anything happen to them so I became very attached. My love for my children was beyond the heavens. I knew inside my heart that had to hold them close.

For a long time Jr. would only talk about how much fun he had in North Carolina and that he could not wait to go back. At this time me and my husband were thinking about selling our home in Maryland and moving somewhere else to give our children a better life.

The neighborhood that we lived in was not the greatest and we wanted our children to be safe and not in danger.

We talked about selling the house for a while but we had no clue where we were moving to. My mother told me that her and my step father was moving to North Carolina and that she wanted me to move there with her and Jr. was also excited and wanted to move there to.

It took about a year and then it was time for us to go. We sold our home in Maryland and moved to North Carolina. We settled on our home December/1/2005. The children seemed to be happy with the new home and I was happy with the location because I knew that the children would be safe here.

It took us three days to completely move in and get settled. It was time for me to put the children into school. I left early in the morning to find the school to enroll the children.

It took a while but finally I found it. They were enrolled that day and were ready to go to school the next day.

After the first week I was seeing a change in Jr. and it was unlike anything I had ever seen in Jr.. Jr. was never a mean child but I starting to see anger and frustration. By the second week I knew that there was something really wrong and it was time for me to find out what was wrong with my child.

I sat down with Jr. because it made no sense to me that he was lashing out with anger because I knew that was not something that Jr. had done before. He had told me that the children in the school were saying bad things to him and that they were hitting him. I told Jr. that I was taking him to school the next day and I was going to talk to the teacher and the principle.

When I got to the school to call the meeting the principle said that I had to talk to her about the problem that Jr. had with the other children. I told her what was going on with Jr. and the other children and she told me that she had to investigate what Jr. was saying and that she would get back to me the next day.

I waited for her response the next day and she never called me. I thought that it was wrong that she never called me because this matter was very important to me that this matter was taken care of as soon as possible.

I decided to call the school and ask why I have not heard from then on the problem that my son was having. They told me that the principle would call me soon.

Weeks went by and there was no call. I was very concerned and worried about what Jr. was going through in school with these other children. There was a big change in my son and I didn't like it. I also knew that as a mother I had to do something about it.

I decided to not call the school I was just going to go there. When I went through the front door of the school there were children in the hall changing classes. As I started to walk down the hall way headed toward the office.

I could hear the children using bad language and to my surprise there were teachers standing there and they said nothing to these children. The children were not quiet in using this bad language and I knew that the teachers heard just what I heard. At that point I knew that there was something very wrong with this school and that my children did not belong here.

I turned around and left the school. I went to my car and called directory for surrounding schools in the area. I knew that I had to get my children out of that school before something happened.

I went to the nearest school which was really far away so I could take my children out of there. When I got to the school I knew that this was a much better place for my children. They told me that they would not accept my children in their school because of where we lived. I was not too happy about the things that were going on with these schools.

I told them the things that my son was going through in the other school and still they would not help by accepting my children into their school.

After a few months of living here I started to get to know the people next door to me. I was telling about the problems that I was having with the school. She asked why I didn't take my children out of there and put them into the other school and I told her what they had told me.

I could not believe what she told me next.

Her child was going to that school and it was a very good school.

She was twenty feet from my house and her child was allowed to attend that school and my children were not allowed.

I felt lost and alone. There was nothing I could do to help my son and what he was going through, our life in North Carolina was not going nearly as well as we expected.

Our children were not happy as well as we were not happy.

Jr. was the one I was most worried about he was being mentally abused and physically abused. As a mother I could not help my son. The school was in control of my children and they were doing nothing to help me or my child. Jr. would get off the school bus crying mostly every day because he was being beat on constantly. I called the school and demanded a meeting because I was tired of the abuse and seeing Jr. in pain mentally and physically.

A few days later I was at the school ready to speak my peace on my son's behalf.

I asked the principle why she didn't contact me when she told me that she would. She then told me that there was no need to call me because my son was a liar and I knew my son and he was not lying.

I told her that Jr. never lied and everything that he said was the truth that the children in her school were abusing my child and it had to stop. She then told me that her children in the school did not like people from the north and that's why Jr. was being abused.

I could not believe what I was hearing. I asked her if she had lost her mind that I have never heard such a thing. She said too many children do not like Jr. because of where you're from. I knew that she was the one lying that the principle knew that Jr. was being abused but she was taking up for the other children in the school.

When I left the school after the meeting I knew that there was no help for me or my son.

They were also abused on the school bus but I knew that I could control that part of the abuse by taking them to school and picking them up.

Some of the abuse did stop and Jr. was a little relieved but the abuse inside the school did not stop. My other two children were in the lower grades and they didn't go through what Jr. was going through. Children were mentally abusing them but they were not being physically abused so I would talk to them and tell them that those children did not have good upbringing and they did not know what they were.

I had told Jr. many times that he should not lash back at these children because two wrongs don't make a right and he was better than that. I was always afraid that Jr. was going to want to abuse other children and think that it was ok to do that. I never wanted my son to hurt anyone but I always knew that a person can only take so much abuse and then they would turn on that person and start abusing them.

I took the kids to school one day and I was talking to a parent and she had told me about a mentor that would be with Jr. all day in school and that would also protect him from the abuse I was more than happy to hear this information about this mentor because I knew that this would stop the abuse on my son.

I called the same day and was set up with an appointment. The next day I was called to the school because Jr. was sick and they wanted me to get him and take him home.

When I walked through the front door I heard someone screaming at someone very loudly and when I turned the corner I could not believe what I was seeing. A child was up against the wall and a teacher was in the child's face screaming at him. When she turned and saw me she then turned to the child and said go to class.

These teachers were creating monsters and I believe that this might have been the reason these children were lashing out at others.

I started to see bad things that I would never thought would go on inside a school. For me to know that the teachers were treating the children like they were nothing and I know that the other teachers herd it as well as I did and we were in front of the office. This is what made no sense to me. I thought that maybe they were physically abusing the children.

I was hoping that I was wrong about that but I was still going to talk to Jr. just to make sure that they were not beating on him because of the bruises that he was coming home with. I think that if the teachers were hitting on the children. They were too scared to tell.

I left the school with Jr. and we had a talk on the way home and Jr. told me that the teachers were not touching him but they were constantly screaming in his face and telling him that he was fat and stupid.

I called the board of education for the second time about the bruises on Jr. and they said for the second time that they would get back to me the next day. I did receive their call the next day and they told me that the principle of the school said that Jr. was hitting his self and the principle saw him do it.

I told that man that he was out of his mind that his principle and his teachers were abusing them children and I saw it with my own eyes. I also told him that if Jr. was hitting himself then how did he produce bruises up and down his back and when I said that to him then he said this conversation is done and he hung up the phone.

Mentally abusing a child can destroy their life forever. The teachers are there to use there intelligence to teach a child and have respect for the child so the child wants to learn. A child only learns what it is taught and if the child only sees mental abuse then that is all the child knows. This is what makes a child lash out at others. If a child is abused the he will abuse someone else.

It was now soon time for the mentor to be with my son throughout the school day.

After the first week with the mentor the abuse started to slow down. I started to see a little change in Jr. but not much of a change because he still had anger for the teachers and the children in the school.

After about three months of the mentor I was starting to get phone calls from the mentor and she told me that we had to meat because there was something that she had to tell me. We didn't get to meet for about two weeks because she had other children that she was mentoring.

We finally met and she told me that the teachers were saying unthinkable things to my son. One of my sons teachers were telling him that he was to fat to be in school and he should stay home where the food is. She also told me that the same teacher asked my son if she gave him food would he do his school work. I knew that Jr. was shutting down and not doing school work because of the way he was treated.

Another phone call I had received from the company that the mentor had worked for and the man on the other line said I know that you don't know me but I am calling you on a matter that happened with your son Jr. He said to me. I was talking to your sons mentor and she told me that she wanted me to call you on this matter and it is very disturbing.

He said that a teacher had grabbed my son by the shirt and pulled him out of the lunch line and they refused to feed him lunch that day. He told me that he wished he could help me in this matter but it was out of his hands.

I never understood why everyone was so afraid of these people and no one would stand up to the principle or the teachers. At this point my son had completely shut down and refused to do any school work.

There was no way that my son was going to do anything for these people that were abusing him. My son was being destroyed by these people and getting help for my son was helpless.

I had one friend that worked in the school office and she told me several times that she did not approve of the things that were going on in the school but there was nothing that she could do.

I was very tired of every person that knew about my sons abuse told me over and over that there was nothing that they could do to help me because they would be fired. I just wanted to keep my child home from school but I knew that if I kept him home I would be in jail. Jr. was starting to get suspended from school because he was starting to fight back with the children but when they were hitting on Jr. and I was complaining about the children abusing Jr. they were never suspended.

I knew that to be true because I was at the school a lot and seen the same children the next day. I always tried to teach my son that no matter what do not fight back because he was better than that. My son was totally transformed from a good child to a problem child.

I received a call from the mentors company saying that Jr. was going to get a new mentor because his first mentor was leaving to another school. These teachers and children were doing these things to my son in the presents of the mentor and the teachers were not afraid that she would turn them in to the police because they knew she wasn't going to do it or she would lose her job.

When Jr. came from school he always went to his room and stayed there all evening and night.

He would not have dinner with his family and when it was time to go on trips with me and his father. Jr. never wanted to go. I think that Jr. was hiding from everyone including his self.

Jr. was holding all of his thoughts and emotions and feelings inside and the only time he would let it out was through anger. And he would release it any way that he could and on anyone at that time he just didn't care.

I could never get my son the help that he needed for the mental abuse that he was going through because the medical that he had didn't pay for it and I wish that I had the money to do it but I didn't.

The pain as a mother that I was going through because my son was being mentally and physically abused by these children and teachers of this school and there was nothing that I could do about it was very heart breaking for me.

Jr. weighed more than a normal child and that was most of the reason why they made fun of him. Anyone that got to really know my son Jr. that really wanted to be his friend or showed him that they cared about him. He would let them in his life and he showed them the real JR..

They loved my son for the person that he really was and the teachers and the ones that cared about Jr. knew that he was very smart and a sweet loving child but we all knew that there was a reason that he was shutting down and that was because of the mental abuse.

The physical abuse was coming to a stop because Jr. was fighting back. The mental abuse never stopped. Sometimes I was even hard on my son because the school work was not being done. Jr. needed to be back home in Maryland with his friends and family and that would have turned my son completely around for the best.

My son needed good guidance and love in his life from everybody around him not just from his parents. Jr. had a good life of happiness until we moved to North Carolina.

All that was taken away and shattered and the child lost it all in a matter of time do to disrespectful people. It all starts at home with the children in how they carry themselves in the world and how they respect others and in this case they had no respect for any one not even there selves. I can't speak for the teachers because they were supposed to be respectful to a child and they had no respect for their self or any other child in that school.

The children have learned this behavior at home and in school and my son was the one child that had to endure this behavior

My son was now moving on to middle school and I thought that things would be different because the children would be older and I thought that he would make friends now and there would be no more problems.

I wanted my son to be happy while he was in school and that he wanted to learn and that he would get along with the teachers and he would find a teacher that he could get close to and that would change Jr. for the better.

Things would only stay the same with the teachers wanting to continue to mentally abuse my son and call him bad names and the children wanted to fight with him.

I decided that I wanted my son to leave North Carolina for two weeks to get away from all that he was going through. School was getting ready to let out for the summer and he was headed to Virginia with his god mother.

He was really happy about going with his god mother and she was very happy to have him.

Jr. and his godmother were very close. Even though they were so far apart they loved each other very much and they kept each other in their hearts.

Days later Jr. called me and told me that he was having the time of his life and he really didn't want to come home.

He wanted to stay with his godmother and go to school there but he could not do that because she had to have custody and I wasn't giving my child to anyone. I didn't have the money for legal papers and to give custody of my son would have killed me. I would never have given any of my children to anyone I could not live with myself if I had done that.

Jr. had his two weeks of fun and now it was time to come home. He spent the rest of his summer in the house because there was nothing for him to do. We lived in the woods far away from anything. He was not happy that he had to come home and I think that made him worse because he was not able to do something that made happy and would change his life and Jr. knew that if he moved with his god mother that things would change in his life and he would not have to deal with mental or physical abuse anymore.

When he was in Virginia for two weeks he met friends that liked him and he found friendship in them. When it was time to go back to school he didn't want to go and he would give me a lot of hell and saying that he wanted to live with his god mother and he never liked this place and that he knew that things were going to get worse.

I think that JR. wanted to make things worse in school because he did not want to be there. Six months into the school year things were really bad for JR.

I think that Jr. wanted to be thrown out of school so that I would send him to Virginia.

I knew that he had to stay there until school let out again and then maybe we could think of something that would help my son and all his problems.

All of my sons problems started from the first day I put him into that school from the age eleven until now and nothing ever changed for the better it always got worse for my son.

I received a call from school one day that my son had been in a fight with another child and the vice principle told me that my son was the cause of the fight.

When Jr. got home from school he told me that he did not start the fight that the other child started the fight. I believed what my son had told me because when he did start the fight he told me that he was the one that hit the child first so I knew that he was telling the truth.

A few days later I was at the school a saw a friend of mine that had a child that was going to that school. She told me that the day that Jr. had the fight with the other child and was thrown out of school. She was there in the class with her son and saw the fight start and Jr. was not the one that started the altercation.

She saw the other child hit my son in the head and then my son hit him back.

I asked her if the teacher was present while this altercation was going on and she said that the teacher was watching it unfold and did nothing.

The teacher lied on my son and said he started the fight and that's why the blame was put on my son. She told me that several times before she saw other children hitting my son while he was walking down the hall way of the school and she noticed the teachers were seeing this happen and were doing nothing.

My son was going through a lot while in this school and they're the ones that destroyed my son.

Jr. was a lost child in his own troubled world and he knew that his mother tried everything to help him through.

There was never a day that went by that my son did not know that his mom and dad didn't love him.

Jr. always knew that we were there for him and that we were never going to stop fighting for him.

In reality my son in his heart knew that the reason he became so angry in his life was because of the people out side of his family. Jr. came home from school and told me there was going to be a new principle in the school.

I was relived that there was possibly going to be a change in that school. The elementary school principle and the middle school principle along with the vice principal were all leaving.

The schools were connected together and I thought in the beginning that would be trouble.

All the children from the middle school and the elementary school were all riding the school busses together.

The big children were with the little ones and I don't think that any parent agreed with that. Just as I thought. Things would get better in the school with the abuse toward the children because the new principle would not stand for bulling.

The mental abuse was not as bad as it was and I learned that if the teachers did something that wasn't right.

She would make sure that it was taken care of. Many times I heard a teacher that they did not like that principle. I liked everything about her because she cared about the children and she changed the school for the better. My son told me that he liked her a lot and that him and her became close.

She would always call me when harm was brought to my children or something just wasn't right. The teachers had to change their ways or the principle was going to find out there lies. I had frequent talks with the new principle and she knew all that was going on at past time with the school and my son.

She made it very clear that if anything had happened involving my children that she would do a full investigation and she would not point fingers unless it pointed to that person.

She made it clear that there would be no bulling in her school.

If she found a teacher that was not doing their job by helping a child or they were lying about a altercation and she found it out that there would go before the board and she would take it to the fullest.

I knew that I could trust her unlike the others because I knew that she meant every word that she said about bulling.

After getting to know her we became good friends and we spoke a lot about Jr. and about my thoughts on things that he was going through inside and the thoughts that she might have.

We tried to come up with a way that would help Jr. and the things that he was going through. She would try to talk to him sense he liked her and maybe he would open up and tell her things that he would not tell me.

I knew that he would not open up to me because he knew that I worry a lot about him and he didn't want me to know all that he was going through.

He always told me that I worry too much and there was nothing wrong. Jr. wasn't going to tell me anything.

As a mother we all know when something is going on with our children. We know when there is more and they're not telling. Sometimes we do so much for our children that they don't want to bother us with their troubles or their thoughts.

When us as parents have unconditional love for our children and they know that you do so much as a parent to protect at child or children they don't want us to worry any more or protect any more than we do.

As for myself I learned that through my son Jr. He knew that I was always there for him no matter what I had to do. My children came first in my life and that was something that I knew no one could take from me. The love for my children was very strong my Jr. knew that. Jr. was my first-born and was the happiest time in my life.

He showed me the way of life and showed me the love that I never knew. Jr. was everything that I ever wanted and needed in my life.

Before the birth of Jr. I was a drug attic and an alcoholic. I lived on the streets and no longer cared about life. I was a abused child and teenager through my life and all I wanted to do was die.

I met my husband by the grace of god and still all I wanted to do was get high to get rid of the pain that was in my head and the drugs was the only thing that would loosen that pain that I was going through.

When I met my husband he had never done any drugs or been in any trouble in his life.

After a while of putting up with me and the things that I was going through he wanted me to get help and he wanted me to be his wife.

I tried to get clean on my own and I thought that it would work. I was still craven the drugs. We decided to go out for the day because he thought that it would clear my mind. I wanted to get something to eat but when I ate the food I became really sick.

He asked me if I could be pregnant.

I told him that I wasn't sure but I very well could be. We went to the Rite Aid and bought a test. When we got home I found out that I was pregnant. A feeling of joy overwhelmed me and at that instant I knew that I had to make sure that I never did another drug. I went to a drug program to get clean but I had to do seven days in and two years out.

One month after I found out that I was pregnant. The man who I knew would love me for the rest of my life we were worried. I knew that my life was whole now and that's all I needed was for me to have something to love.

Things were going really well in my life. The excitement of getting ready for the baby to arrive was very strong and I could not waiter to hold my child and say to someone else look what I have created and he belongs to me and no one can take that from me.

When Jr. was born it was the happiest day of my life. In the hospital I wanted him to be with me at all times.

When the doctors were to take him to do varies things to make sure that he was ok.

I felt like they were taking him from me but I knew in my heart that they were bringing him back.

My mind would run crazy and I would think that they would get my son mixed up with another child and I would not get my son back.

I was very protective over my baby and I wanted no one to touch him. Jr. was a wonderful baby. Growing up Jr. had a lot for a child and he was very much loved and everyone around him wanted to shower him with anything that he needed or wanted.

When Jr. had Christmas there was no room for anything else. He was a child that never wanted for anything. There was nothing in the word that he ever needed or wanted because he had everything.

When I was a child I never had Christmas and nice things that a child needs.

I lived on the street a lot because my father was an alcoholic and he stayed in bars until his money was gone.

My father never cared about his children and on Christmas morning when we woke up and seen that the Christmas tree had no gifts we were told that we were too bad so Santa never came.

I wanted to give JR. things that I never had but most of all I gave him love and that was something that I never had when I was a child so I found myself giving everything that I didn't have to Jr..

I didn't want my son to go through life without knowing that his parents didn't love him.

Jr. was a fine boy with dreams of becoming a game designer and wanted to go to Japan to do it. Jr. had other dreams of being a bounty hunter.

He always had a lot of friends. It seemed like every child that he met they would like Jr. and wants to be his friend. Anyone that knew him could tell by the joy full child that he was that a person could only love him.

Anything that we done for Jr. he was happy that we did it but Jr. was never selfish.

He would wrap up a toy of his and give it to one of his friends at Christmas time.

I never understood why or how a teacher could treat a child with disrespect or even how they would expect a child to want to learn in school being treated like anything other than a child.

A child grows up learning what they a taught and a child takes in everything.

When a child is taught disrespect then that is what they do and that is how they treat other people. A child with anger is a child that does not want to learn and they start feeling different about things in life.

They will not get along with others and the anger gets worse. Jr. started to take his anger out on others in different ways. He would come home from school so angry and he would hit the wall. Jr. would go to his room and cry and I would hear him yell and he would say bad word to his self hoping that I would not hear it but that was imposable because I always heard everything and it broke my heart to know that my child was going through hell.

Jr. was never like that he was always a good separated child and got along with everyone. I thought by moving my children that things would be really good for them and that would mean even better then when we lived in Maryland.

My son was lost and many times I tried to dig deep inside of him and pull out of him what was wrong and he would not give me anything.

The happiness and joy of a child can never be taken from that child. If it is taken away it can destroy a child and it can destroy his or her out look of life and all the good things in life mentally.

A child is given life and put on this earth to bring us joy and laughter.

When that child is hurt inside it changes everything for the child and us as parents.

And sometimes as helpless as things seem we have to be there for our children so they won't completely give up in life.

A child only dreams of love from others and their dreams in life.

Life is to short as we know it and we have to cherish every minute of every second with them because they are counting on us and without us they will never know the way.

Our children are our future. We have to stand up for our children and never always believe what someone else tells you about your child unless you have investigated the matter yourself. Us as parents know our children better than anyone else and us as parents have to stand tall for our children and always let our children know that no matter what we will stand for them.

Children can sometimes deceive us in not telling the truth but we know the children better then they know themselves and we surely know the times when they're telling the truth.

Never the less the measurement of our love for our children will never decisive the outcome of our decision.

Jr. was a very delightful child who never deserved the way he was treated and the loss in interest in life that he had and started to believe that he was nothing and never would be nothing.

He said many times that he didn't care if he made something of his self because he thought that he was to fat and no one would except in any area of the world because of it.

Is loss of interest to him to a whole another side and a whole another way of things that could be true in his life and give him the happiness that he deserved but Jr. just didn't believe that it was possible any more. All his thoughts and hopes were taken from him. Life is very deceiving to all of us and no knows what the outcome of our life could be but it's always good to keep your wishes and dreamed alive and to always believe that they will all come true and nothing can stand in our way. What would we do without our children running our future?

We depend on our children and grandchildren. There was never any hesitation with me wanting to help my son in any matter that he might have had with the school or any of the teachers. There was never anyone out there to help me or my son.

They would all lose their jobs. The sickness for them to be tormented to scar them to be in danger to lose their jobs. If they spoke on my behalf there only means of liven came to a end.

I will never know how these people must have felt knowing that they could not help me or my son because of being threatened. They told me many times that they wanted to help because they knew that what was happening with Jr. was wrong and something had to be done.

I was always there for my son no matter what he needed me for he always had his mother. In 2009 Jr. was going to be transferred to the high school because they thought that it would be good for Jr. and that he was to old to be in middle school.

I wasn't happy at first because I knew that Jr. wasn't getting his education. They were pushing him off as they did in the past. Jr. was happy about the transfer because he was going to high school and the children were older. I think that Jr. thought that things would be better for him because he had hopes of making friends.

The first month in the high school Jr. was real excited about being there. He was starting to talk about being a game designer and a bounty hunter or maybe even a plumber like his father.

I thought that his excitement of life and all his dreams were coming back to him.

Just when Jr. was getting excited about his life again and the things that he would have liked to do. it was all taken away again as it was in the past.

The kids in the school was starting to hit on my son again. They were using language that I could not believe that would come from a child.

Jr. was all interest again. He was staying in his room and sleeping all the time and wanted to do nothing.

I could see his life going downhill again and at this point I was getting angry with all the people around me it didn't matter who you were I hated you because I was hurt inside that there was nothing that I could do and Jr. was going through hell in his life.

Before long he was being suspended from school for defending his self from the other children. I knew that the physical altercations would start before long because he told me that it was time that he defended his self from the children and the teachers.

Jr. was done with it all and he was not going to stand for it any more.

The rest of the time that he was in the high school he did hit back and he never held back.

On February 10/2010 Jr. was going to be sixteen years old and he was talking about leaving school and not going back.

As a parent I was upset because I wanted my son to finish school and make something of his self because my life was destroyed by abuse and I wasn't able to stay in school and make something of my life.

Jr. told me that there was no hope in getting these people in trouble and making them pay for what they done to him that there was only one way for him to get away from it all was to leave school and to never go back.

Not many days after his birthday he left school and he told me that he was sorry but he could not deal with the abuse no longer and that one day he made a promise that he would go back to school and get his G.E.D.

After a week or so there was a change in my son's attitude. He was a much happier child and I noticed him to want to go outside and do things and wanted to go over his friend's house and he was the only friend that Jr. had.

Jr. loved to make things out of wood and he loved to shoot a gun with his father. Jr. and his father did many things together on weekends when his father did not have to work.

Jr. loved to play ball with his father and his two brothers. He might not have been getting his education like I wanted him to but he was much happier and he wasn't being abused.

My son was happier than ever but he still did not like North Carolina. Jr. always enjoyed reading books and he was helping me study some test so I could get my G.E.D. My son was very smart but he would never use it in school. He would only use it intelligence for certain people.

When his grandparents visited us on weekends Jr. always enjoyed their visit. Him and his grandfather would joke with a lot of laughter and he always wanted to help his grandmother because he thought that she was too old to do anything.

Most of all C J was very close with his grandfather. When he was a little boy he would call his grandfather uncle poppy but the love that Jr. had for him was unstoppable and could never be crushed by anyone.

Jr. and his father were also very close and their love for each other was also unstoppable. He always looked up to his father and to Jr. there was no one that could take his place.

JR. meant the world to all of us and we loved him very much.

When Jr. came into this world we were all given a gift. For two years I was writing a book and in January 2010 my book was completed and it was my sons dream to get it published. I was really happy that the book was completed but Jr. said to me many times. Mom don't worry because one day it will be published. He was always more worried about me then his self.

I have always tried to influence Jr. to do his best in life because we only have one chance at what we could do. I wanted him to get his education and to never leave school. I wanted my son to the winner not a looser and by Jr. leaving school the children that was abusing him would become the winner.

I would always tell Jr. that these children should have no influence on his life and I always wanted Jr. to be strong and never let anyone to stand in his way. I didn't want Jr. to let the abuse overcome his life because it would be another life wasted and destroyed.

My life was all about abuse and my future was taken and still to this day it bothers me and I will never forget the things that I went through as a child. No child will ever forget trauma that has happened in their life.

I wanted Jr. to block out the abuse and try to do his best but then again I always knew that it was imposable to do because I could never do it. Things would always get worse when I tried to forget.

I think that it was too late for Jr. to forget and that is why he gave up and there was no way that he was going back because Jr. knew that things would be the same and there was no hope for a change.

My son always had pride but the pride that he had was always crushed. He would build it up and then it was always take away and I think that he didn't want to rebuild it anymore.

Jr. was wonderful child any many took that from him and turned him away at a time of need and that made him loose all interest in everything.

After leaving school Jr. tried to find a job but that was always a letdown for him because nobody would hire him. Everything that my son tried to do. he was always letdown.

There was no reason for Jr. to hank on any more or even dream about what he could have been he thought that it was time to let go and move on.

He wanted to leave North Carolina and to never return because he hated everything about this state and as far as he was concerned the state of not Carolina took everything from him and everything that he could have ever been.

Jr. was sixteen years old and never used drugs or alcohol and he hated cigarettes. He was a really good boy and yet he never had a chance to stay in school and no would ever stop the abuse that he was going through.

The only reason my son got as far as he did in school was because there was three teachers that loved Jr. and tried to help him through.

The rest of the school was always no good for my son and they didn't care that what he was going through because knowing that they were wrong they always took up for the other child.

They hated my son and wanted to destroy his life. I had many talks with my sister over a few weeks about Jr. going to live with her and maybe he would go back to school and get his education because Jr. went to school there for two months one year prier and he had many friends and no abuse and his grades were excellent but the only thing was I had to give temporary custody but if that's what it took for my son to live a good life and make something of his self then that's what I would do for Jr.. I had not talked to Jr. at this point but before long we would talk and see how he felt about things.

I knew deep in my heart that he wanted to go with his god mother but I would not let him go until he made me a promise that he would go back to school and make good grades so he would have a good life.

I wanted Jr. to work hard toward his dreams in life and make it happen. I wanted my son to be the winner and show the world that he could do it because I didn't do it.

I loved my son and I knew that it would break my heart to see him go but something had to be done for him and I knew that this was not all about me it was more than that and I had to let go.

As a parent I was hurting inside because I would not know what to do without my son by my side and I could no longer see him grow to a man and I could hold him and tell him that I loved him unless it was on a phone and that was going to be the hardest thing in my life.

I knew that we would not have the money to visit him because my sister lived so far away and it would be hard for us to get there.

I didn't work and the money that my husband made wasn't enough to pay our bills.

On the third week of May 2010 I talked to Jr. about going to live with his aunt and going back to school and making something of his self and he was very excited and he could not wait to go.

He was set to go on June 4/2010. It was only a couple of weeks away before it was time for Jr. to leave and I was feeling sick because it was hard for me to let him go.

My children are my life and for them to leave me whether it be with a family or somewhere else it hurts.

My mind was going a thousand miles a minute and I didn't know what to think next but when I talked to my husband and he told me that Jr. needed some breathing room in his life because of all that he has been through and that Jr. would be ok and better off in Virginia.

I started to feel a little better about things and I thought that maybe I needed to let loose a little because he would be ok and he needed a change.

The week before it was time for Jr. to leave for Virginia my brother called and said that he was coming to pick Jr. up and take him to my sister's house so that I didn't have to take him because my brother knew that I really did not have the money and he knew that I would be taken it from a bill to do it. I really wanted to spend the last week with my son before he went to Virginia but Jr. was happy and wanted to leave then.

I told my brother that it was ok to come get Jr. and take him then. On Thursday my brother called me back and said that it had to wait until Friday June 4/2010.

He had to work and could not take off because if he did he would lose his job. I told Jr. and he was not happy but he said that was fine that he would wait. Jr. loved his aunt which is also his god mother so much that he would have waited a life time to be with her.

I sometimes think that he was closer to her then he was me because he always had the deepest love for her.

I always knew that he loved me to but he was so close to his god mother that there was nothing that could ever tear them apart.

My mother and father wanted to visit Jr. before he went to Virginia because it would be a while before they could make the trip to Virginia to see him. They were coming over on Sunday to spend the day. We were going to have a cook out and watch movies. JR. always loved to see his grandfather because his grandfather was a lot of laughs and him and Jr. would joke together and watch movies JR. loved nothing more than to spend time with his grandfather even if it was for a minute. His grandfather was also his heart. When they arrived the last Sunday of May 2010 for their visit we all ate very well and Jr. and his father and grandfather were in the living room watching a movie.

They were joking and laughing like many times before.

They had a good time with each other and JR. was happy that day to be with his dad and his grandfather. The next day which was Monday morning Jr. told me that his throat was hurting and his mouth was dry and I thought he was coming down with a cold so I gave him penicillin that the doctor had given to him left from not long before for being sick and he said mom I am going to lay down and maybe I will feel better and he said to wake him up for dinner.

I told Jr. that I would have dinner ready when he woke up.

A couple of hours latter Jr. came out to eat dinner and I asked him if he felt ok and he said that he felt much better.

I wasn't worried because he looked better and he was eating but I noticed that he was drinking more than normal but I didn't think anything of it because I thought that it was because his throat was hurting and that his mouth was dry.

We went to bed that night and everything was normal.

When I woke up five o'clock the next morning on June 1/2010.my husband told me that Jr. was up a lot during the night and he thought that maybe Jr. was really sick beyond what we thought he was and he needed to see a doctor.

JR. came into the room and was talking to me and his father and I told JR. that I was going to run his father to work and I would be back to take him to the hospital.

He said to me. Mom I am getting a shower and I'll be ready. I returned home about eight thirty quarter till nine. On this day there was no sense of time and my whole life was shattered and crushed.

When I came into the house I called for Jr. but there was no answer so I turned to go to his room and he was coming up the hall way but he was falling into the walls.

I noticed that Jr. wasn't dressed and ready. I said Jr. why aren't you ready and he said mom I am dizzy and I am really sick.

I told Jr. to sit on the couch wile I changed real quick and found him close.

I went to my room changed and got his cloths and when I came back into the living room Jr. was sleeping and I told him to get up and get dressed but he had no strength.

At this time I was scared because I didn't know what was wrong with him so I helped him get dressed and I put his shoes on and I told him to stand up and let's get to the truck.

He was yelling at me to wait and was talking things that I could not understand.

Finally he stood up and when he did my son hit the floor and the whole house shook. I was scared to death. My son was not responding to me and I tried to lift him but I could not get him off the floor. I called 911.

During the wait for emergency to get there Jr. was in and out of it and he was talking to me. I was so afraid for my son and at the same time I had no understanding why he was so sick because he was talking to me fine when I left but when I returned he was very sick.

Before the emergency arrived my son asked me if I had all his stuff ready for the trip and did I buy his drinks for the trip and I told him that his cloths were ready and I would get his drinks before Friday.

He was set to leave in three days. When emergency arrived they were not prepared because they had to go back out the door to get there medical bag and then the heart monitor.

My son was laying on his stomach and so they turned him over and put the heart monitor on him but then they started C.P.R. on JR.. I noticed that my son had a heart beat so I turned and looked at the paramedic and he said something but I didn't hear him because it sounded like I was in a tunnel. I think I was in shock. I turned and looked at the heart monitor and my son no longer had a heart beat.

At that point I just started screaming and asking god to please take me and let Jr. live. I fell to my knees and prayed for him not to hurt me this way and asked god what have I done for you to take my son. The paramedics took the monitor off my son and took him outside on a stretcher.

I went out behind him and told him that I loved him. When I touched my son I knew that he was gone and there was nothing anyone could do for me or my son and that's how it has always been since we moved to north Carolina.

The paramedics took my son to the hospital. Me and my husband wasn't far behind. When we arrived at the hospital a nurse to me and my husband to a room where we met with the doctor. The doctor was asking us several questions about Jr. and finally my husband said to the doctor is my son dead and the doctor finally said yes.

I went back to tunnel hearing again and I started screaming. The nurse said that I had to calm down so I could go in the back to see my son one last time.

It took a few minutes to calm down enough to my son. We went to room that they had my son in and when I saw him laying there lifeless if felt like the whole world was falling down on me.

I could not believe that my baby boy was now gone. Me and my husband were in disbelieve and I didn't want to except the fact that my son was no longer here.

I grabbed my son and didn't want to let go and I was crying so hard. My tears were falling on his cheek. Someone had put there fist through my chest and pulled out my heart and crushed it and a piece of me was gone forever.

There is nothing in this world that could ever replace my son and the love that we shared for each other. It was time for me to walk away from my son and when we entered to hall way I thought about my other three children who were waiting to see if there brother was ok.

At this point there was no way that I was going to let them see their brother's lifeless body laying there because I knew that it would destroy them mentally forever.

When we went back to the waiting room to our other three children I did not know how to tell them that their brother past away because it would be the hardest thing I could have ever done. They wanted to go see Jr. but I told them that they could not and there was something that I had to tell them.

All they were saying to me was mommy is he ok please let him be ok.

I held my children and told them that Jr. was gone that he was with god now in a better place and they started screaming and crying.

I walked them outside to the truck so me and my husband could talk to them more. They were crying so hard and there little bodies were trembling. We all cried together and me me and my husband told our children that we loved them very much and we were sorry that Jr. was gone.

All of our lives were crushed. We loved Jr. very much and now he was never coming back. We put the children into the truck and started heading home.

On the way headed home something was telling me to go back to the hospital to see your son one more time because you're never going to see him again. I told my husband to turn around. When we arrived back to the hospital my mother and father was there and so was there preacher from there church and he was praying over my son.

I wanted nothing more than to see Jr. get up off that bed and go home with me but I knew in all reality that wasn't going to happen.

I leaned over my son and told him again that I loved him and I we would never forget him. When I looked up at my father he looked like he was going to pass out and I asked him if he was going to be ok and all he said was.

What happened to my grandson we had a good time on Sunday and I don't understand. He leaned over Jr. and kissed him good bye.

I knew that we had to leave because one of us were going to really break down and someone was going to get sick.

We all went home to grieve over Jr. and for days I could not sleep because every time I closed my eyes I would see my son lying on that hospital bed lifeless.

Then I knew that I had to prepare myself for the funeral and that was going to be so hard for all of us.

Jr. was cremated so I could bring him home and keep him forever. His services was going to be in a church and all friends and family were going to be there.

Some of the teachers and principle from the middle school that cared about Jr. came to his services. They cried and showed that they really cared about my son and I wasn't surprised because I always knew that they cared for Jr. but they really showed it when they came to show their respects. These teachers and principle will always mean a lot to me because they didn't only care about Jr. they also cared about me and my other children.

They will always be number one in my heart as far as friends. If one day I ever leave the state of North Carolina I will never forget them and I will always keep them in my heart. I will always remember the good that they have done for me and my children because before they came along there was no one that cared.

The day of the funeral it was hard for all of us and we had a big loss in our lives. The preacher was the best he would only talk about my son.

The ceremony was all about my son and nothing more it seemed like he knew my son all along and that he really cared for Jr.. He will also be in my heart forever and I will never forget him as long as I live. I could not have asked for more every person that came that day showed their love for my son even if they didn't know him.

After the ceremony the church had food for everyone that came but not all stayed and that was fine with me because they came and there love and that meant the world to me Everyone that helped with my son's funeral and all who gave donations will also be in my heart forever.

I will never forget anyone that was there for Jr.. The family was together but a lot of the family in Maryland was not there because some of them didn't know when or where the services were and some just could not come. Everything happened so fast we forgot to tell them when and where.

I feel sad about that and I wish I could turn back time and I wish my son was still here with us. Our family has always been close to one another and I wish they could have been there for Jr.. From the beginning things things weren't good for none of us the loss of Jr. turned my world around and I can't change that.

Our family is still close but we have all learned that we have to cherish every moment with our children and each other. Life is to short we have to spend every wakening moment letting each other know that were there and to hold on to each other's love because what if there were no tomorrow.

After the funeral I was receiving cards and letters from family and friends. I was receiving letters from people that I didn't even know telling me how sorry that I lost Jr..

Me and my husband never thought that so many people cared but yet there was so many people that did care and that touched my heart in a big way that I can never explain.

During the time of receiving all the cars and letters I was trying to be on the road to recovery and I found out that I was never going to recover from the loss of my son. There isn't a day that goes by that I don't cry for Jr..

My son was sixteen and yet he slept with a teddy bear every night and now I sleep with his bear. There isn't a night to pass that I don't have his bear next to me.

Jr. was always an awesome kid and in his eyes. His mother always came first in everything. One day I will see JR. again to be with him for eternity and no one can take that from me. I was really hard for me and my husband to wait for the test to come back on our son and we thought that it was taken to long.

I called the hospital and talked to the doctor that was doing all the test and she told me that she was almost done and in a couple of days she would send it to me.

About three weeks after talking to the doctor I finally received the papers in the mail and I reason why I wanted them so bad was because the paramedics that were at my house on June/1/2010 tried to say that Jr. was alcohol and I knew better but I was in a rush to prove them wrong.

Jr. never used drugs or alcohol he was a good child and a pleasant child and no matter what they said about Jr. I knew that they were lying. They were very rude when they entered my home and they were also not prepared.

When a paramedic has to go back out to their truck to get a medical bag and a heart monitor that to me means that they were not prepared to save a child's life.

At that point I knew that they had no care in the world for my child and the attitude with me was because they thought that my son had consumed alcohol and I was that was buying it.

They were proved wrong and they have to live with that lie every day because my son was clean and always has been. They also said that it only took twenty three minutes and I know better than that because we waited longer then that it was about a forty to forty five minute wait.

My sons life I think could have been saved. They lied about the time of arrival just like they lied about my son consuming alcohol. I had to watch my son die before my eyes and all they did to save their self was lie. I deal with the heartache every day that maybe Jr. could be here today if they arrived sooner because the whole time waiting for them to arrive Jr. was talking to me.

They said when they arrived here that Jr. was responsive to them and they lied about that because he was already in a diabetic coma. I have consulted a firm and it is there word against mine and because they stopped C.P.R. after so long it would not have saved my sons life.

I don't believe it. I think Jr. could have been saved if they arrived sooner and if they would not have stopped C.P.R.

My thought is because they work for the state that's the reason they got away with it all. As a mother I will consult another firm because I will never be done fighting for Jr. he is my son and I will not give up on him or the fight.

I was here that day on June 1/2010 and I know what happened and I won't let them get away with the lies that they told. I know how long we waited and I know what happened that day. I will take my story as far as it needs to go and it's all for Jr.. I have never let my children down in the past and I will not start now. I will go to my grave fighting for Jr..

It has been four months and I still cry every day and the worst part is yet to come. The holidays and his birthday is coming and every day that goes by is still like the first day when he passed away.

My heart will never be whole again. I have always told my children and stuck with every word of it that I will always be there for them no matter what.

The fight for Jr. will never be over and his name will forever live on. I get frequent visits from my son. Several people in the family experience paranormal.

Jr. will touch us and he will show his self to us. I have heard him calling my and many other things have happened inside and outside my house. My husband was driving up the road early in the morning and my husband got cold as ice and then the truck shut off while he was driving. My husband looked down at the dash board of the truck to see what was wrong and when he looked up a huge bear about eight hundred pounds was in front of the truck and as the bear past my husband tried to start the truck and it started right up and we have never had a problem with the truck since.

My son was there to save his father's life and no one can tell us any different. If my husband would have hit the bear at sixty miles an hour he might not have lived. When my husband told me what happened I knew that Jr. was there with his father. Jr. is our guardian angel and he watches over all of us. My sister always sees my sons spirit mostly all the time because that is where he wanted to be.

He was very close to his god mother and she was his heart. It doesn't matter what anybody thinks I talk to my son all the time and I know that he can hear me. Me and my sister talk a lot about the good time we have had with Jr.. There is times we laugh together and times that we cry together.

When Jr. was visiting her one year before he passed away. Jr. would tell her that he missed his mom and could not wait to see her and that made my day to hear that.

As I think back to the beginning of when I first became pregnant with Jr.. My son was a gift from god because when I found out that I was pregnant with Jr. my life was saved. I was an abused child from the age of six until I was twenty two.

My father was an alcoholic and a drug attic and he physically and mentally abused me. I had turned to drugs and alcohol to get my father out of my head because he lived there every minute of every day and my only way out was to get high.

I met a man that fell over hills for me almost instantly. We were then married and had a beautiful child. My life was changed forever.

Jr. lived a good life with his family and was loved very much but he was abused by others and not treated by others as a child should be. My son was bullied by children and adults inside the school that he attended.

He was a good child at one point in his life until we moved from one place to another and I watched my son slowly lose interest in everything that had to do with his life and his future.

I lost a part of myself and I will never be whole again. I struggle every day with trying to deal with the fact that my baby boy is never coming back. I have no understanding why and can never find answers. My beautiful baby boy has left me and took my heart with him. I ask myself. What did I do wrong for my son to be taken or what did he do wrong to lose his life. I will never have a answer but I never thought that forever would be to say good bye to my son so soon. I loved Jr. with all my heart and soul and every day I have only one wish and that would be for my son to return back to my arms where he belongs. Jr. is the reason that I am here today and JR. is the one that saved my life but there was nothing that I could do to save his life.

I would have giving my life for Jr. to be alive today and I would do that for any of my children. I have laid my son on a bed of roses and gave his spirit to Jesus. Jr. never had a chance at life and he lived a short life of no time at all and all his dreams were shattered.

None of us ever thought that we would ever say goodbye to Jr. unless it was one of us leaving. The loss of Jr. has broken a lot of hearts and nothing can ever replace him.

One day I will be with my son again and we will fly free together and I will find my son when I go to heaven and I will knock on every door inside the mansion until I find him but when I do. My heart will be whole again. Jr. is now my angel and I know that he watches over me every minute of every day and my love for my son will go on and the love from others will go on and Jr. will never be forgotten.

Many people who have treated my son the way that they did has felt pain inside when Jr. past away. I seen changes in people at my sons funeral and when I visited the school one week later I noticed that people were crying that mentally and physically abused Jr. there was a difference in people and I think that they were heartbroken that Jr.. was gone and they were hurting because of the things that they did to Jr..

Because what if there was no tomorrow and we didn't have the chance to say sorry and maybe give a hug to say we were sorry. Sometimes it is too late for things to change and that's why we need to cherish each other at every minute of every day because we may never have a second chance.

I knew that those people were very sorry for what they did and I forgave them because I knew that my son would have wanted me to do that if he would have had the chance to see what I did and if he could have seen the way that these people were so heartbroken over him.

I know that Jr. would have forgiven them. Life is too short to hate and we need to learn to love because we are all family. We have to love our children and show them to care for others and to never hate because we all only have one chance and once that chance is gone there is no more.

Jr. was a wonderful person and if they only gave him a chance they would have loved Jr..

I think that Jr. taught a lot of people a fair lesson about life and he taught them that we can't undo what is already done. I have been in the school several times since the passing of my son and I don't see the things that I have seen in the past and the children and the teachers that my son never got along with say high to me with respect and that tells me that a lesson was learned.

A lesson of life and love and that it doesn't take a lot to learn it and as far as I am concerned Jr. will live on through a lot of people. Our children are our future and we need to teach them well because there is one chance and I will teach my children the one chance and how to love and care and not to hate and I want them to know to dream and carry on them dreams because life is good.

All I have left is my sons smile and knowing that people were not nice to him and still he was strong and held his head high and he refused to give up. My son had a heart of steel and it was broke many times but he always picked up the pieces and put it back together.

He never once wanted to worry me about the things that he was going through. Jr. was strong at heart and loved his family. He was a awesome boy with a lot of dreams that were crushed by short life. The short time that I had with my beautiful son I will cherish for the rest of my life. I will never forget his beautiful smile and his beautiful eyes and his joyful ways. Jr. had his own special way about his self that was very unique. He had a touch that would warm anybody's heart. Jr. always cared for others and put his self last no matter what. Selfishness never had a place in his heart and his mother and brothers and sister always came first.

Jr. lived a short life but he will never be forgotten. He has left us with his memory and his love and he has forgiven others for the wrong that they are sorry for he was good child who should have lived a longer life but he was a child that filled us all with love and touched our hearts with his smile and he is now a touch of an angel.

He is happy to see a change in others and he is watching today with a smile and his head held high. Jr. was a wonderful child filled with a lot of love that had a heart of gold. He will never be forgotten.

Jr. 2/10/94
To 6/1/2010 IN LOVING MEMORY